FRANCE
COLORING BOOK

This book belongs to:

_____

_____

Color And Learn

Enjoying this book?
Please leave a review because we would love to know your thoughts, feedback and opinions to create better paper products for you! Share how you creatively use your notebooks, journals and stationery products.
Thank you so much for your support.

Arc de triomphe

Cartoon-musketeer

Cathedrale notre dame

Champ the mars of paris

Charles de gaulle

Chateau de versailles

Coat of arms of french kings

Coat of arms of jeanne darc

Death of robespierre

Eiffel tower

Emblem of the french republic

Flag of île de france

Fleur de lis

France map

French football federation logo

Gare de lest

Gilbert de lafayette

Great bastille

Great seal of france

hotel des invalides and the grand-palais

Jacques cousteau

Joan of arc burning

Joan of arc

King louis xvi

Louis pasteur

Louis xiv

Louis xvi threatened by the mob

Luxembourg garden

Maximilien robespierre

Medal of the legion of honor

Mont saint michel

Mont parnasse tower

Moulin rouge

Napoleon bonaparte

Notre dame

Notre dame de paris and pompidou-centre

Queen of france

Rousseau

Sacre coeur basilica in montmartre

Sacre coeur

St genevieve

Storming of the bastille

the arc de triomphe and la defense

The arc de triomphe and madeleine-church

The eiffel tower and champ de mars

The eiffel tower and champs elysees

The louvre

The louvre

The louvre museum and the seine river

The palais garnier opera and moulin rouge

The pantheon and latin quarter

The trocadero

Voltaire

Young marie curie

Made in the USA
Monee, IL
31 May 2022